LUCKY

A CHILD'S DREAM
COME TRUE

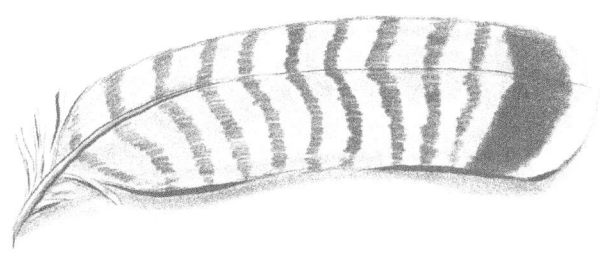

BY STEPHEN A DARRETTA

ILLUSTRATED BY
DANIELLE DARRETTA CANNON

Lucky: A Child's Dream Come True

Copyright © 1998 by Stephen A. Darretta

ISBN: 978-0-578-26113-3

Check us out on Facebook

or online at

www.luckythehawk.com

Special thanks to:

Cathy and Sieg Gengl for the years of making my story into a book.

Michael Darretta for the original editing.

Anthony Darretta for the original illustrations.

Joey Darretta for reading it to many classrooms.

Danielle Darretta Cannon for the updated illustrations, and edits.

In Memory of
Anthony Darretta and Fred Basciano
Two men that left us way too soon.
This book is dedicated to you.

TABLE OF CONTENTS

CHAPTER 1

HELP

Chapter 1 – "Help!"

A peal of thunder roared across the black sky. The heavy rain danced wildly against the muddied wall of the steep cliff. The cold wind seemed to cut deep into the face of the young boy. He held tight to the weakening branches of the battered bush. His body shivered both from cold and fear, a fear that he could not hold on much longer.

"Help!" he called out, barely able to hear his own voice. "Help me!"

Gathering a deep breath, the boy screamed again. The thunder and rain screamed louder.

"Can anybody hear me?" he cried meekly.

The young boy hung tight to the bush; the one thing that kept him safe from the deep below. He could not see the bottom, but he knew it must be hundreds of feet down. He tried once more to pull himself up.

Crack!

The branches began to give way. Panic gave way to instinct as he quickly repositioned his right hand and pressed his body against the rocks. The weight of his body was more than the bush could hold. He blurted out a bone-chilling scream that echoed endlessly down to the cliff's floor. More sounds of cracking twigs delivered the frightening message that time was short.

Sobbing uncontrollably, the boy tried to call out once more. Again, the laughing thunder mocked the boy and scolded him to keep quiet.

The boy knew his cries would never be heard. There was only one hope. He needed to position the whistle into his mouth.

But he dared not let either hand go free.

CHAPTER 2

HAPPY BIRTHDAY

Chapter 2 – "Happy Birthday"

Staring through the living room window at the evening sky, Jimmy sat dreaming of the day ahead. His father gently tapped him on the shoulder and motioned that it was time for bed. He tenderly carried the boy upstairs to his room where Jimmy's mother was waiting. She had his bed ready, knowing full well that her son would find little rest in it. Jimmy's father entered the room and laid Jimmy on the bed. He tickled the young boy under his cheek. Jimmy giggled.

"Put your glasses and your whistle on the nightstand son," said Mother.

Jimmy put down his glasses, then pulled the whistle from his neck. He always wore his whistle for protection. If there was trouble, he would blow.

Jimmy's parents tucked him into bed, bent over and kissed him good night. Father reminded him that tomorrow would be his birthday. Jimmy giggled once again, and a smile grew on his face, exposing his missing two front teeth. His big brown eyes exploded with joy, anticipating the big day.

"Close your eyes and go to sleep, Jimmy," whispered Mother. "You have a big day ahead of you tomorrow."

"But Mom, I can't. I'm so excited."

"Now, son, remember...," reasoned Father.

"But I can't sleep, Dad. I can't stop thinking about getting my very own pet."

Jimmy had no brothers or sisters to play with. So, for his seventh birthday, his parents promised him that he could have the one thing he always wanted. They promised Jimmy his very own pet.

"The sooner you go to sleep, son, the sooner tomorrow will come," said Father.

With that, the room darkened as Jimmy's parents said goodnight. Jimmy turned his head and gazed out his bedroom window towards the moon that shined upon the top of Devil's Mountain. His face aglow, Jimmy's thoughts were far off in the distance, filled with visions of dogs, cats, rabbits, lizards, snakes, and fish of a thousand colors, as he slowly drifted to sleep.

* * *

The sun peeked through the bedroom window and danced upon Jimmy's freckled nose. His flaming red hair blazed like fire in the sunlight. The warmth of the sun upon Jimmy's pale face woke him. The big day had arrived. It was Friday morning, and school was closed for teacher's meetings. He had been asleep no more than a few hours, yet his eyes popped wide open.

Grabbing his whistle from the nightstand, Jimmy blew it harder than he had ever blown it before. The high-pitched shriek caused Jimmy's mother to leap out of bed, and she hurriedly made her way through the doorway. In great panic, she bounded up the long staircase and quickly flung open Jimmy's door.

"Jimmy, what's wrong?" cried his mother.

"It's my birthday, Mom! Let's go to the pet store right now!"

Mother let out a sigh and shook her head. She glanced at Jimmy's clock. It was 6:27 AM! "Honey, it's way too early," she said. "Please go back to sleep. The pet store isn't even open yet."

"But Mom, I want to go get my pet."

Jimmy could not go back to sleep. It was like a Christmas morning.

* * *

After a very quick breakfast and a very long morning, the time had come to travel downtown. They arrived at the front of Siggy's Pet Store just in time for the "Open" light to be turned on.

They entered the store, and immediately Jimmy was in his glory. "Whoa!" Jimmy said excitedly as his brown eyes lit up with joy. He was captivated by all the sounds and smells the pet store had to offer.

Jimmy saw puppies yapping wildly, wrestling uncontrollably, and misbehaving as only puppies do. The kittens in the next pen, not to be outdone, were just as wild and excitable as the puppies. Their friskiness was accompanied by a medley of meows.

There were rabbits, lizards, snakes, and fish of a thousand colors decorating the pet store just like Jimmy had imagined.

As excited as he was seeing these animals, Jimmy's attention was curiously drawn toward the back of the store. For some reason, he sensed something was to be found there. Maybe there he would find his birthday present. Jimmy slowly made his way down the aisle toward the back. Mother followed him, wondering where his thoughts were leading him.

They passed through the bird section. To the left were beautiful multicolored canaries with feathers of blue, green, and yellow.

"Mommy, look at these!" cried Jimmy as he stared intently through the bars of the cages.

"They are beautiful, Jimmy. Is that what you want?" asked his mother.

Without an answer, Jimmy quickly turned to the neighboring cages that housed the parakeets, finches, and lovebirds. "Look at these, Mom!" he yelled while he glanced back and forth from bird to bird.

"Do you want a lovebird?"

Jimmy just answered with a small sigh. "I can't decide. I didn't know finding a pet was going to be this hard."

Then, something caught Jimmy's attention. In the back of the store, Jimmy noticed the owner, Mr. Siggy, acting rather odd. He edged closer to get a better look. Jimmy's eyes widened as he moved to the scene. Mr. Siggy was trying to restrain a large bird, a very large bird, frantically defending himself within his cage. A painful scream echoed from the struggle as Jimmy clumsily approached the cage.

"Why are you hurting him, Mister?" Jimmy said with great concern.

Without turning his head, Mr. Siggy answered in a frustrated voice, "I'm not hurting him, I'm restraining him," He bit down on his lip and secured a grip on the bird. The creature tried to battle back, but his beak couldn't penetrate the leather glove Mr. Siggy wore.

"Why are you doing that?" Jimmy asked.

"I have no choice. This bird has to be destroyed."

Jimmy didn't like how that sounded. He quickly turned to his mother and asked, "Mommy, doesn't destroy mean kill?"

Mother looked at him with compassion. "Son, sometimes people need to do things they wish they didn't have to do."

Jimmy turned to Mr. Siggy. "Why? What did he do wrong?"

Mr. Siggy, bothered by the conversation, answered sternly, "He didn't do anything wrong.

He's crippled. He was brought to me with a badly broken wing beyond repair. I don't have the time or the patience to take care of him. He can't take care of himself, and besides he must be miserable. In fact, he's making me miserable. This hawk will never fly again."

As the last few words left Mr. Siggy's mouth, he finally stopped long enough to turn to Jimmy. As he was about to speak again, he hesitated and felt a flush of embarrassment, then shame, as he looked upon the child. The boy's legs were bound with metal braces from his hips to his feet. He supported the weight of his powerless body with metal crutches held firm by each arm.

The young boy was crippled too.

Mr. Siggy turned his eyes away from Jimmy.

Jimmy's face filled with tension. "Mom, I'll take care of him. I want him. Please, Mom. Please? I want him."

Jimmy's mother replied quickly, "We can't take this bird, honey." Her face produced a gentle frown.

Without hesitation, Jimmy said, "Why? Because he's a cripple?" There was a long silence.

Mr. Siggy, feeling quite guilty and embarrassed, looked back at Jimmy. He stared for a moment then asked, "You really want him young man, don't you?"

Jimmy nodded.

Mr. Siggy turned to Jimmy's mother. "I'll tell you what I'll do, Ma'am, with your permission of course. I'll give you this bird, for free. You can have the cage and the leather handling gloves to boot. No charge, just as long as your son takes care of the bird."

"Oh, thank you sir. But we can't ever care for a...a... what is it?"

"A hawk, Ma'am."

"A hawk! We can't bring home a hawk."

Jimmy's mother turned to Jimmy. She saw the look of desperation and disappointment on his face. She realized then that this bird already meant quite a lot to her son. But she also knew they had better settle for the lovebirds.

"Jimmy," she replied, "let's go back to the lovebirds."

"But Mom," Jimmy said, "you promised."

Jimmy's mother remembered the promise made just a week ago. Jimmy could have any pet he wanted. Her focus then turned toward the hawk. She stared intensely at him for a few moments and became intrigued with the hawks piercing eyes. The white speckled markings on his chest formed a shapely diamond that complemented the blend of black and red-brown feathers. Even though his sharp, curved beak and massive talons gave an air of fierceness, they did not dampen the beauty of this majestic bird.

18

"He is beautiful." Mother confessed.

"Mommy," Jimmy replied, "I want him."

His mother smiled and with her hand caressing her son's red hair. She then turned to Mr. Siggy. "Okay, okay. We accept."

"Hurray!" Jimmy shouted in victory.

"What does he eat?" Mother asked.

A delighted expression arose on Mr. Siggy's face, "Oh, he eats an assortment of things, like raw meat. And for a special treat, you might go over there and pick out a few mice. He really likes those."

Jimmy's mother groaned. She turned to her son, "Honey, are you sure you wouldn't rather have one of those beautiful goldfish?"

Jimmy just looked at his mother with a huge smile and glowing eyes. She knew she was beat.

"I'm telling you right now, son. I refuse to feed him." She too began to smile.

"Yes!" he cried, and the other animals seemed to applaud. The joyful little red headed boy turned to the fortunate bird and shouted, "You're coming home with me."

Jimmy's mother turned to Mr. Siggy and said with a gracious smile, "Thank you so much for making my son's birthday so very special. You're a good man."

"Ain't nothing 'bout it," answered Mr. Siggy. "Besides, I really do hate to see any of my animals destroyed. This one in particular, he's... well, he's kind of unique."

Mother glanced strangely at Mr. Siggy as he walked toward the front of the store. With that, Jimmy, his mother, the hawk, and three mice left for home.

On the way home, Jimmy asked his mother, "What should I call him?"

"I don't know, Jimmy. Whatever you like," said his mother as she reached over and lovingly stroked his hair. "All I know is that this bird was very fortunate that you came along when you did."

"Mommy, what does fortunate mean?"

"Fortunate means lucky."

Jimmy glanced at the back seat where the hawk stood perched in his cage. "Lucky...Lucky. I'm gonna call him Lucky."

CHAPTER 3

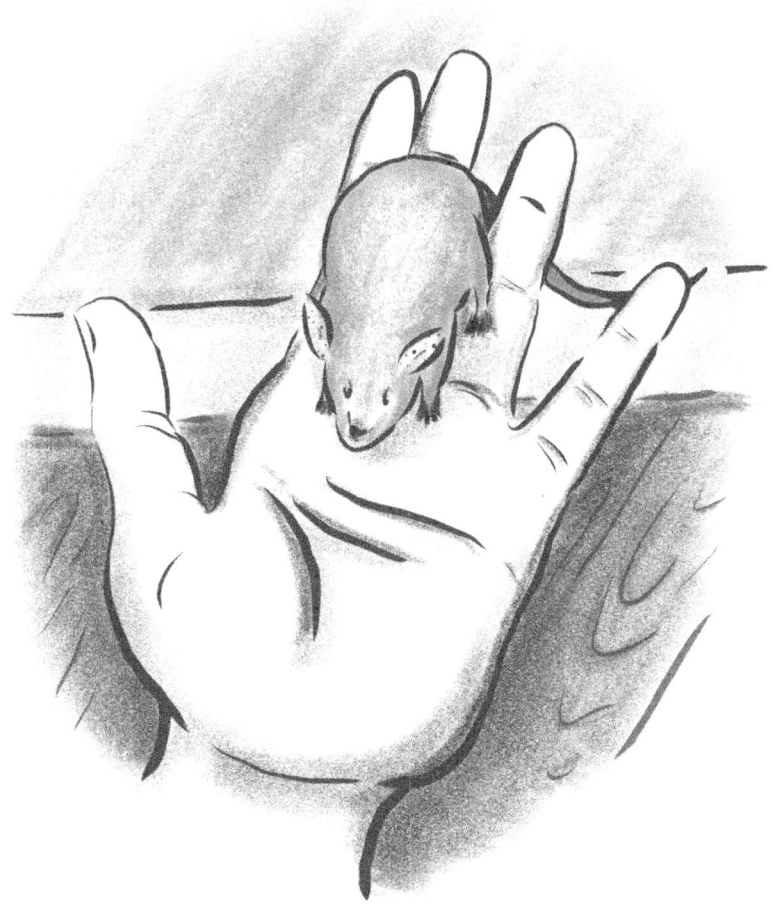

AN UNPLEASANT SURPRISE

Chapter 3 - "An Unpleasant Surprise"

"Mommy, do you think Daddy will be surprised?" Jimmy asked, feeling a bit worried as his mother parked the van and prepared to enter the home.

"Surprised? Oh yes, very!" Mother answered. She couldn't stop thinking of how her husband would feel about this new member of the family.

Mother lugged Lucky and his cage into the kitchen and placed him on the dining room table. Jimmy trudged slowly behind. Mother glanced over to the answering machine and noticed the red light was flashing. She reached over, pressed the silver bar and continued on with her business. The tape rewound, and a familiar voice greeted the family.

"Hi, Honey. Happy birthday, Jimmy! Just wanted to let you know I'll be home earlier than expected, and I can't wait to see the fuzzy little furball you picked out. Be home soon."

Jimmy's mother just chuckled and shook her head as she thought to herself that little does he know, the only little furballs they had brought home were Lucky's special treats.

Mother went upstairs, leaving Jimmy to spend a few moments with his new friend. Jimmy edged over to the cage and took his first long look at Lucky. He marveled at the beautiful diamond painted upon Lucky's chest. He inspected the sharp talons and wondered if they could penetrate the leather handler gloves given by Mr. Siggy. His sharp upper beak stretched long below the lower beak, undoubtedly able to tear apart the toughest of meat. Jimmy then looked closely at Lucky's left wing. The wing seemed shorter than the other, partly because it was slightly crooked from the break near the middle. Finally, Jimmy saw Lucky's eyes. The dark pupils seemed to penetrate deep into Jimmy's own eyes, as if the hawk was checking him out. Lucky's eyes seemed to tell Jimmy that this was not your ordinary hawk.

Suddenly, they both heard a hard scratching. The familiar sound distracted Lucky and startled Jimmy. Lucky balanced himself on his perch. A step to the right, a step to the left and back again. Lucky's nervous movements and piercing eyes were directed toward the cardboard box near the cage. Jimmy understood what Lucky wanted.

"Mom, I think Lucky is hungry," Jimmy said.

"Give him a piece of last night's steak in the fridge," Mother yelled from upstairs.

"Can he have one of his treats?"

"Forget it, Buster."

Sadly, Jimmy told Lucky he couldn't give him a mouse. But then, with cunning known only to a seven-year-old, Jimmy bent over and whispered, "I can't give you a mouse, Lucky. But Mom didn't say I couldn't show you one." Quietly, Jimmy reached for the box and gently dragged it in front of Lucky's cage. Jimmy then gingerly lifted each flap of the box. As light entered the opening of the box, the scratching of the mice frantically intensified until, suddenly, one of the little prisoners made its move. Taking advantage of the small opening, a small gray, speckled eared mouse quickly leaped from the box, fell to the floor, and scurried across the kitchen.

Jimmy let out a startled "Ah!" and Lucky let out a frightened shriek. Boy and bird were both visibly shaken. Jimmy was afraid of what Mother would do. Lucky was afraid he had lost his lunch!

"Mom! Mom! He's getting away!" screamed Jimmy as his mother ran down the stairs. She was all prepared to find Lucky out of his cage and perched on top of the hanging light. She gathered her nerve, expecting to lure him down with a piece of raw meat. Instead, she ran into the kitchen to find Lucky securely in his cage.

"What's wrong?" Mother inquired.

"Look!" pointed Jimmy.

The little mouse dashed across Mother's feet. Immediately, she let out a horrified scream and in one jump leaped to the top of the kitchen counter. Her feet tightly tucked safely underneath her.

Just then, the front door swung open, and the words, "Happy Birthday!" trumpeted past the entryway and echoed throughout the house. Jimmy's father was home.

"Daddy! Daddy! Get 'em! He's getting away!" The frantic voice forced Father's smile to give way to an uncertain frown. Expecting the unexpected, his alert eyes carefully scanned the entryway toward the living room. A step, a pause; a step, a pause. Then, without warning, two ounces of fur darted from the corner of the entryway and scurried directly through Father's legs.

"A mouse?" Father laughed. Of all the pets in the world – dogs, cats, hamsters – his son had chosen a mouse. The proud dad knew that his boy was a chip off the old block. He had barely told Jimmy about Aristotle, his own pet mouse from his childhood. Aristotle was the best mouse in the world, and Father had never quite gotten over his tragic end with the new Hoover vacuum cleaner.

Father used his boyhood skill and quickly, but carefully, sneaked up on and grasped the little creature with his callused, yet clean, hands. Father looked keenly at the new family member and quickly calculated what to name the new pet. Squeaky? Nah, too common. Sheba? Nah, too trendy. Beethoven?

Jimmy made it to the living room in time to witness the mistaken union of his father and the varmint. He sighed with relief.

"Dad! You got 'em!" He said happily.

"Oh Jimmy," Father replied proudly, "I never thought..."

Mother calmly came off the counter. She wondered if anyone had even noticed her plight. With a little smirk of embarrassment, Mother called for her husband. "Honey," she inquired, "would you please step into the kitchen?"

Her husband gently held the little mouse in his left hand, caressing it with his thumb. "Cute little thing," Father whispered. He put his right arm around Jimmy's neck, smiled, and headed toward the kitchen to offer his congratulations to his wife. Aristotle? he wondered.

With one foot in the kitchen, Father's smile froze.

Lucky, as well as any hawk knew, offered his greetings. He squawked.

"What!?" bellowed Father.

Father's left hand betrayed him, and the little mouse fell to the floor. The mouse squeaked, Mother screamed, and she jumped on Father's back. Mother's arms wrapped tightly around Father's neck as the mouse scampered about his feet. Father hopped as he skirted the mouse.

Mother screamed, trying to balance on her husband. Jimmy began to chuckle.

"Please get off me, Honey!" Father pleaded, trying to be both courteous and practical. Mother screamed again.

Finally, Father's feet skirted one time too many. The mouse ran off free into a dark corner, and Jimmy's parents tumbled to the floor. Mother braced herself with her hands and averted danger. Father fell forward toward Lucky's cage and instinctively grabbed hold of it. Jimmy closed his eyes as bird and man came crashing to the ground.

Father shook away the cobwebs. He turned his head to the right to look face to beak with the most unwelcome sight he had seen all week.

Lucky, recognizing that the previous greeting did not go very well, decided to try it again.

"Squawk!"

Father frightfully jumped back into the kitchen cabinet. Jimmy and his mother began to laugh hysterically.

CHAPTER 4

WELCOME TO THE FAMILY

Chapter 4 – "Welcome to the Family"

"We can't have this...this...hawk," Father said. "He's not a pet. This is a wild creature!"

Lucky stood inside his cage next to the entryway. Jimmy sat alongside Mother on the couch. Father paced back and forth on the grey carpet. He held a pencil in his hand, as was his custom during family discussions, although he never wrote anything.

"He's not a wild creature," Jimmy said.

"Jimmy, you need to understand," Father reasoned. "This is not a dog. It's an eagle."

"A hawk," Jimmy corrected him.

"Okay. A hawk. You see, you can't just go to the pet store, pick out anything that moves, and—"

Just then, Mother interrupted. "Honey," she said, "do you remember our promise?"

Father stopped as if frozen.

Mother continued. "Jimmy saw the hawk was injured. He couldn't fly, and Jimmy felt...well, he felt sorry for him. Anyhow, he is quite beautiful."

"Beautiful? I think tigers are beautiful, but you don't see any tigers in our backyard."

"Oh, come on, honey. Just look at him. Really look at the bird for a moment."

Lucky, as if understanding the plea, began to demonstrate some of his remarkable characteristics. His evenly layered feathers ruffled, seemingly doubling his already large frame. The stiff plumage on his head raised to its full splendor, as if being crowned. His diamond-shaped chest marked his claim to royalty like a coat of arms. Above all else, Lucky's intense and piercing eyes captivated Jimmy's father.

Father looked back at Jimmy and Mother. He attempted to mutter a few syllables, but nothing intelligible came out. Lucky continued to stare.

"All right! I guess the bird can stay for now," Father said reluctantly. "But I'm not promising anything. If this doesn't work out, he's going back to the store. No questions asked."

Jimmy and Mother smiled. "Why don't we take him upstairs to your room?" Mother asked Jimmy.

Mother lifted Lucky's cage and led Jimmy upstairs. "By the way," she said to Father, "don't forget to find that mouse!"

Father saluted and said, "Aye-aye, Captain!" At that, Father began peeking around for the little furball.

Mother and Jimmy entered the bedroom and placed Lucky on the stand next to the window.

"Mom," Jimmy said, "will Dad make us take Lucky back?"

"Don't worry, honey," she answered, "your father will soften up soon."

* * *

The long, thin tail of the mouse extended out from underneath the closet door. Father crept on his knees, ever so closely, ready to pounce on the rodent.

"Honey?" Father was suddenly startled. The tail vanished. Mother stood behind him.

"Did you find the mouse?" she asked.

"Well, sort of..." Father said sheepishly.

"Anyhow, Jimmy's all excited about going to the library to gather books about hawks. I thought you might like to take him."

"Okay. But I'm telling you, if this hawk is any trouble--"

"I know, honey. Now you and Jimmy just go along and have some fun. I'll finish getting ready for tonight's birthday party."

* * *

Open books were sprawled across Jimmy's bed. Colored pictures of birds of prey covered the plaid, goose-down comforter. Eagles and falcons, but mainly hawks, decorated the covers of the borrowed library books. He learned that hawks were bigger than their cousins, the falcons. He also learned that eagles were rarely kept as pets, and one type, the bald eagle, was the national bird of America. He read that hawks would feed on a variety of insects and smaller animals, including birds, rodents and reptiles. Lucky looked like a red tail hawk, but Jimmy was not quite sure. Maybe it was because in Jimmy's eyes, red tail hawks were the most beautiful of all hawks. He read that wings of a hawk are called sails, claws are known as pounces, and the leather handling glove that Mr. Siggy gave him was called a gauntlet. Saturday cartoons suddenly seemed unimportant. Jimmy was engulfed with his new love.

That evening, Jimmy's birthday party sort of went as planned, more or less. Jimmy had the neighborhood kids over, and it almost took an act of God to tear those inquisitive youngsters from the barred cage that sat next to Jimmy's bedroom window. The kids were awestruck by the massive talons and razor-sharp beak Lucky had. The kids listened intently as Jimmy talked about Lucky, and all the amazing things he had learned about hawks in only one day. Neither a birthday cake nor presents could draw their interest from Lucky's cage. But despite all, the kids kept asking the same question over and over again: "When is Lucky going to eat the mice?"

When the party was over, and the kids departed. Despite their excitement, they were disappointed not to witness the gruesome assault of a predator upon its prey. But even this did not dampen the unusual spirit that Lucky brought to Jimmy's birthday party.

That night, Jimmy did not bicker the least bit about going to bed. Bedtime meant time alone with Lucky. Both parents kissed Jimmy good night as they tucked him into his goose-down comforter, shut off the lights, and left.

"Hey Lucky, we're both covered with feathers," said a tired and silly Jimmy, giggling.

* * *

The dripping of the coffee pot signaled the new morning. Father fetched the newspaper while Mother was finishing the scrambled eggs. Father tossed the paper on the kitchen table and leaned over to his wife.

"You know, it's a rare occasion that you and I can spend a quiet moment together like this," he whispered.

Suddenly, a whistle shrilled, breaking the silence.

Jimmy was awake.

"There's something wrong," Mother replied, alarmed.

The two hurried to the staircase, and as they grabbed hold of the banister, they stopped... they began to hear the sound of laughter.

A squawk came from Jimmy's bedroom, and then a whistle in reply. More laughter followed.

Father turned to Mother. "Those two are having a shouting match!"

Lucky squawked again. Jimmy replied by blowing his whistle.

"You know," said Mother, "I don't remember seeing Jimmy so excited in...well...for as long as I can remember."

Jimmy blew his whistle once more, then called out for his parents. They slowly climbed the stairs and opened his door. Jimmy's toothless smile greeted his parents.

"Dad, we need to hurry and go back to the library."

"Jimmy, the library isn't open at 6:30 in the morning," Father said. "We'll go later today. Just try to go back to sleep. You too, Lucky." Father closed the door, shaking his head in disbelief as he realized his household would never be the same again. Mother tried to hide her smile, then broke out in a childlike chuckle.

"What's so funny?" Father remarked.

She laughed. "That boy has no intentions of going back to sleep."

Jimmy blew his whistle. Lucky squawked back.

CHAPTER 5

PIGEON BOY

Chapter 5 – "Pigeon Boy"

The afternoon bus ride home was especially warm for Jimmy. Not only because of the hot sun gleaming down on his shoulders, but because it was the last day of school and the first day of summer!

As always, the bus stopped in front of Jimmy's house. The driver helped Jimmy down the two steps to the sidewalk in front of his home. After he was safely down, she waved, wished Jimmy to "Have a great summer", and drove off. Jimmy waved back and watched the bus turn the corner. Now, he thought to himself, I can get on with more important things. Like feeding Lucky.

He was headed for the front door when something caught his attention. Looking up, he noticed a bird flying overhead... it was a hawk! Hawks were not rare in this part of the country. Yet, Jimmy was far more interested in them now than ever before.

So that's how Lucky would fly, Jimmy thought with excitement. The hawk was flying toward the field near his house. Jimmy turned to the front door, then stopped. He knew that he should never head toward the field alone. But he really wanted to watch this hawk up close.

Jimmy heard the vacuum cleaner upstairs. *Mom will never even notice*, he thought. Besides, at seven, he figured he was old enough to take care of himself.

Jimmy moved toward the field. It was only a football field's length away. Clop, clop, clop, went Jimmy as fast as he could on his crutches. He noticed the hawk hovering around a particular spot. He wondered how Lucky would look flying in such a fashion.

Jimmy was but twenty feet away from the field when the hawk appeared almost to stop mid-flight. Jimmy got more excited and moved faster toward the field. Suddenly, the hawk dove down toward a grassy meadow beyond the rocky perimeter. Jimmy's eyes widened as the hawk descended rapidly to the grass. Jimmy stopped to watch as the graceful bird swooped down and ...

Jimmy's heart skipped a beat. The hawk returned to the air with something small and gray between his talons.

"Wow!" Jimmy yelled.

"Bet your stupid hawk couldn't do that," said someone behind him.

Jimmy shut his eyes. He knew that voice. He knew it all too well. Martin Winslow was only eight years old, but he was built like a ten-year-old. He also had a heart about as soft as a baseball bat.

"What's wrong?" Martin sneered. "Are you tired of taking your pigeon out for a walk?"

Jimmy turned around. Martin was a few feet away on his bike. "He's not a pigeon. He's a hawk."

"A hawk? A hawk that's as lame as you are," Martin laughed.

Jimmy knew better than to start something. He clasped his crutches and began to move back toward the house.

"Wait a second," Martin said. "Don't you know that it's cruel to keep a lame pigeon? Why don't you just give it to me and I'll put it out of its misery."

Jimmy new Martin's intent. Martin always liked to be the big shot, the bully. Now, he was playing second string to a hawk. The whole neighborhood loved to see Lucky. He was the talk of all the children.

"Just leave me alone," Jimmy said softly as he tried to move away from Martin.

"Hey!" Yelled Martin as he grabbed Jimmy by his shirtsleeve. "That pigeon of yours should be shot. And as for you, I need to remind you who's the boss around here."

"Let me go." Jimmy grabbed for his whistle.

"Oh no you don't." Martin pulled the whistle off Jimmy's neck.

"Ouch!" Jimmy was now more angry than scared. "You give me that back!"

"Do you want it? Then go get it."

Martin threw the whistle into the open field.

"See you later, pigeon boy," mocked Martin.

Jimmy stared angrily at the hard-nosed kid as he disappeared around the corner.

"That Martin," Jimmy growled to himself. "I'm not as lame as he is."

Jimmy began to head back home, thinking Mother would find his whistle. Jimmy knew he should never go into the field alone, and his mother would not be happy with him if he did.

I can find that whistle, Jimmy thought, *Then I can go home and see Lucky and everything will be okay.*

Jimmy edged back toward the field. It was a short walk yes, but he had never been there alone before. As he neared the field's perimeter, he saw the rocky steps that led to the grassy meadow. Jimmy saw a reflection flicker from the grass.

"My whistle!" he exclaimed happily.

Jimmy moved quickly toward the grass. A squawk startled him. He looked to the right to see the graceful hawk atop a nearby telephone poll.

"So, you stopped to watch me," Jimmy said laughing. "Well, you can snatch a mouse, but I can snatch a whistle."

Proudly, Jimmy neared the grass. He then saw the rocky step. The step was about two feet high. He only needed to clear this one to be in the soft grass. Jimmy stopped at the rocks and became frightened.

Jimmy looked at the hawk. "I bet you know Lucky," Jimmy said. "Do you think he'll fly someday?" he asked the hawk.

The hawk stared off in the distance. He did a short dance on the telephone poll, then settled down.

Jimmy laughed. "I guess that means yes." He looked down at the step. "Here goes nothing."

Jimmy moved his right crutch slowly to the bottom of the step. The crutch touched the ground. Then, with care, Jimmy began to inch his right leg down. Success! The hard part was done.

The hawk's silhouette startled Jimmy as it darted from the pole and flew directly in front of him.

Frightened, Jimmy lost his balance and stumbled off the step. His left knee came crashing down on a bottom rock. "Oh!" Jimmy cried. His knee felt like a hot coal. A trickle of blood began pouring down his leg.

I need to get up, Jimmy thought with fear. He tried, but every move caused a sharp pain to rush through his body. The glistening of the whistle caught his eye. Jimmy no longer cared about getting into trouble. He was in real trouble now.

As fast as he could, Jimmy dragged himself toward the whistle. The moist blood felt warm against his skin. The soft grass, though, helped him glide along slowly. Closer, closer... Then, finally, he reached the whistle. Jimmy grabbed it and began to blow as loud as he could.

"Mom!" Jimmy cried as he blew the whistle again and again.

* * *

Upstairs, Mother was finishing up the vacuuming. The crumbs from Jimmy's crackers were sprinkled across his room. Mother grinned slightly as she vacuumed over them.

Lucky was a bit fidgety. Jimmy should have been home by now. Then, suddenly, something caught Lucky's attention.

"Squawk!" cried Lucky.

The sound of the screaming hawk startled Mother. She put her hand over her heart and glared at Lucky as if to say, "Do you mind?" Mother continued vacuuming. Lucky screamed again.

"Lucky, quiet. No!" Mother yelled.

"Squawk! Squawk!"

"Lucky!" Mother yelled angrily. She turned off the vacuum.

Lucky squawked and squealed and bounced back and forth in his cage. Mother moved toward him to cover the cage with a blanket.

She grabbed the blanket and said sternly, "This will keep you quiet, you loud-beaked —" Mother stopped to hear a sound.

She heard a whistle.

Mother burst through the front door and ran outside to find her son. "Jimmy!" she yelled.

Jimmy continued to blow the whistle. Tears rolled down his eyes as frustration and pain together gripped him. "Mom!" he cried and blew his whistle again.

Mother heard Jimmy's voice coming from the field, and she ran to the field's perimeter. She stopped and saw Jimmy's helpless body lying amid the grassy meadow.

Mother hurdled the rocky steps and ran to Jimmy. "Honey, are you okay? Oh my God!" she said as she saw the blood on Jimmy's leg.

"Mom, I'm sorry," Jimmy said. "I saw a hawk and I wanted to watch it fly and I asked him if he knew Lucky and —"

"It's okay. It's okay," Mother said gently. She picked up her son, gave him a hug and brought him back to the house. "We're headed for Dr. Ambers this minute."

"But Mom, I want to see Lucky."

Mother breathed a deep breath. Her eyes welled up with tears. She wanted to see Lucky too. She wanted to thank him.

CHAPTER 6

A SECRET PLACE

Chapter 6 – "A Secret Place"

"Mom," Jimmy said.

"What is it, dear?" Mother replied, kneeling down as she was positioning bait into a mouse trap.

"Lucky and I are going out for a bit. Is that okay?"

"Sure. But where are you going?" Her attention remained fixed on the trap as she slowly placed it behind the kitchen refrigerator.

"We're going to try to find some bugs."

"Just be very careful this time and don't be too late. And don't go back to that field."

"I won't, Mom, I promise."

Just as Mother was about to let go of the trap, a frightened mouse scurried out from behind the refrigerator and dashed under the dishwasher. Mother screamed and dropped the trap. The spring released, the trap slammed shut, and cheese splattered across the floor.

I want to move, she thought to herself.

* * *

With a smile on his face, and Lucky waddling and hopping at his side, Jimmy set out for his favorite place. Even though it was less than fifty yards from his house, it was a place that no parent would set foot; a place where squeamish kids would run out screaming; a place where only the adventurous dare tread. It was dark, desolate place where spider webs laced the sides of vine covered walls and lizards found refuge under large rocks. Creepy crawlers abound. It was the butterflies' graveyard. This was Jimmy's secret place. There were no friends, no parents, just Jimmy, Lucky, and the surroundings within.

"Here we are," Jimmy said. "Now remember, this time I want to come back with something... so behave yourself." Jimmy lectured Lucky as he was pointing his finger in front of him. Lucky in response just playfully put his beak around Jimmy's finger, not acknowledging a word Jimmy was saying. All he knew was that he was going inside his favorite place also.

It did not take long for Jimmy to find his first bug, and it was a beauty.

"Wow. Look at the size of this potato bug." With his bare hand, Jimmy reached down and picked it up. He placed it in a bag that hung around his neck.

He turned to Lucky. "Now remember, leave it alone."

They ventured further. Jimmy began to move some small rocks with the end of his crutches. A six-inch lizard darted out and sped past Lucky. Lucky, showing all the speed and cunning of his breed, pounced on it.

"You got him, boy," Jimmy said proudly. "Now, give him to me."

Lucky hesitated for a moment, then within a few seconds the lizard disappeared.

"Nooo..." said a disappointed Jimmy.

Lucky smacked his beak a few times, enjoying the aftertaste of his choice morsel.

"Please Lucky, don't eat all the good ones. I really want to bring home something to show Dad."

Within a few steps, Jimmy stopped and glared at a large black spider that spun a web that blocked him from going any further.

"Look at the size of that," Jimmy said.

Showing off his knowledge, Jimmy began to teach Lucky about spiders.

"See, Lucky. We don't need to be afraid of spiders. If they're in your way, you just touch them and they'll move. Watch."

Jimmy may not have known as much about spiders as he thought. The length of the spider's legs and its six large hexagon shaped eyes with two small eyes below signaled trouble. Jimmy was about to poke a soldier spider. A great leaper and the most fearless of all the arachnids. A spider that can jump fifty times its length. To make matters worse, nestled in the rocks next to the web was a beating spider sack. Babies eagerly waiting to emerge. This spider was on guard.

Oblivious to the warnings, Jimmy lifted his right crutch and poked at the spider. After a few pokes, the spider disappeared. Jimmy looked at the end of his crutch. Turning towards Lucky, a confused Jimmy whispered, "He's not there." Slowly Jimmy raised his crutch, moving it ever so slightly.

"There he is." The spider stood motionless at the tip of the crutch.

Suddenly, the spider raced up the crutch toward Jimmy's arm. Jimmy screamed and Lucky squawked as he threw his crutch to the side. Jimmy could not get out fast enough.

Once outside, Jimmy let out a sigh of relief. Lucky slowly trotted out from behind.

"You chicken. Why didn't you get the spider?"

Lucky just smacked his beak again. The aftertaste of the lizard was still there.

"He could've killed me."

Lucky lowered his head into his chest. He looked as if he was pleading for forgiveness.

Jimmy neared Lucky and got nose-to-beak with him. He was about to lecture Lucky when suddenly, Lucky gave him a hawk's version of a kiss.

Tickled, Jimmy began to laugh. He hugged Lucky and said, "Okay, you're forgiven. Let's go. At least I can show Dad my potato bug."

Jimmy pulled the bag from over his head, placed it upon the ground, and opened it. Jimmy could only say one thing, "Lucky, noooo!"

CHAPTER 7

SUMMER FUN

Chapter 7 – "Summer Fun"

"Okay, Lucky. Hold still now."

Jimmy placed oil in the palm of his hand and reached towards Lucky who was comfortably set on Jimmy's bed. Jimmy carefully put the oil on Lucky's broke wing. He wasn't quite sure how it helped, but he had heard that people had done this sort of thing when someone was hurt. Lucky seemed tense at first. But, as Jimmy gently rubbed his wing, Lucky relaxed. In fact, he seemed to enjoy it.

"Now, isn't this nice?" Jimmy asked. "Just think Lucky, someday you're gonna fly. I know you will. In fact, I bet you'll be the fastest hawk there ever was. There won't be a mouse safe within miles of here. Now, just a few seconds more..."

Just then, Jimmy's father knocked on his bedroom door.

"Son, there's someone here to see you."

Jimmy guided Lucky back into his cage and made his way to the living room. There, waiting for him, were Pamela and Charlie, two kids from the block. They waved to Jimmy as he entered the room.

"Is Lucky ready to come out and play?" Pamela asked.

The front yard was filled with kids from all over the neighborhood. Summertime is a time for fun, and Lucky provided the best fun in town. As usual, Jimmy would sit down on the grass and have Lucky set up on his arm. Jimmy always wore his gauntlet so that Lucky would not accidentally hurt him with his talons. Jimmy would then glow as bright as the hot summer sun whenever a boy or girl would come forward to view this wonderful sight. Of course, Lucky was proud too.

"Wow!" Antoine would gasp. "That bird could eat my whole hamster."

"Is he real?" little Jessica would inquire.

"Can I touch him?" Maurice would always ask. Of course, he would only place his index finger on Lucky's back. No one was allowed to touch anywhere near Lucky's beak.

"I gotta go potty," Courtney would say as soon as she came near Lucky. Jimmy wondered why she always waited.

This scene would repeat itself every summer afternoon. This was something new for Jimmy – that is, this sudden popularity. There hadn't been many kids who paid attention to him until now, unless they were teasing him. Now, almost no one teased Jimmy. Lucky and him were the talk of the neighborhood. No one around had a pet quite like this.

"You know, those two are becoming quite the pair," Mother told Father as they spied on Jimmy taking Lucky out for his daily walk.

"Becoming? You never see them apart!" Father said.

"Now do you think it was a good idea for us to bring home Lucky?"

"Yeah, yeah. It's pretty wonderful seeing Jimmy being...you know, so happy. I don't ever remember seeing him so excited. I guess it is a good thing. But you know..."

"What is it, honey?"

"Well, I don't want to be a killjoy, but something's telling me that this can't go on forever."

"Oh, come on, honey. Lucky hasn't been the least bit of trouble. In fact, I'm kind of getting used to him taking care of our son."

"But remember, this is a hawk. People just don't keep hawks like...well, like dogs."

"Dear, you worry too much," Mother said playfully. "Besides, it's not like Lucky's gonna hurt anyone. He's as harmless as a bunny rabbit."

"Bunny rabbits do bite, you know."

Mother smiled and looked back at her son. She knew everything would be just fine. She turned back to her husband.

"By the way," she said. "Have you decided when you two are going camping this year?"

"Us two?" father replied. "I don't think Jimmy could last one day away from that hawk. I think it would be best if we just canceled our camping trip this year."

"But didn't we promise Jimmy that—"

Just then the back door began to open.

"Mom! Dad! Can Lucky and I watch some T.V.?"

"Sure," Mother said. "But don't forget to get ready for dinner."

"We won't. Come on, Lucky." Like a puppy with his master, Lucky trotted along beside his best friend into the living room.

Father turned to his wife and grinned.

"Well, they don't allow dogs at the campsite anyhow."

* * *

Saturday afternoon was business as usual. Lucky and Jimmy put themselves on display for the neighborhood kids to stare in wonder. Pamela, Jessica, Antoine, Charlie and Maurice were all there. Courtney even remembered to go potty first. Lucky was impressed by that. Everything was going just fine until—

"Hey pigeon boy," sneered Martin as he rode his bike on the lawn.

"Oh, hi," Jimmy said.

Lucky eyed Martin with serious displeasure.

"What you got there, a canary? Nah. Canaries fly."

Lucky adjusted himself slightly upon Jimmy's arm. He wanted to be sure he was ready in case there was trouble.

"Lucky's gonna fly someday, you watch," Jimmy said.

"Hah. He'll fly 'bout as soon as you're gonna walk." Martin laughed as he climbed off his bike. Lucky stared directly at Martin.

"Martin," Antoine said excitedly. "Did you see his big claws?"

"They're called talons," Jimmy corrected. "These talons are strong enough to tear apart a whole snake."

"And a person, too" added Antoine.

The crowd gasped in disbelief.

Martin wasn't the least bit impressed. In fact, he was a bit irritated by the whole matter. Being eight, he figured he would be king of this neighborhood for some time. But now, someone had taken over his throne. No, he was not the least bit impressed at all.

Martin looked a Lucky's talons, then glanced at Lucky's eyes. Lucky stared at him with hardly a flinch. Martin knew that there was something unsteady about that stare.

"You think those talons could tear apart a snake? I bet they couldn't even cut a piece of bread."

Jimmy was becoming impatient. So was Lucky.

"Why don't you just go away?" Jimmy said in frustration. Jimmy then grabbed one of his crutches and began to pick himself up. Martin moved toward him.

"Here. Why don't I help you."

Martin lunged forward to push Jimmy down. Suddenly, before Martin could complete his evil deed, Lucky stretched out his good wing and let out a scream that could be heard two blocks away. Martin was so startled that he jumped backward – right into his own bike.

"Whoa," Martin yelled as he tumbled over the bike and landed backwards, head-first on the rear tire. The children laughed.

"Martin! Are you all right?" asked Charlie, extending a hand to him.

"Go away!" Martin blurted with embarrassment. Jimmy could hardly keep a straight face. Martin slowly got up.

"You just stay away from me and my friend," Jimmy said. Lucky nodded in approval.

"You wait, pigeon boy. You're gonna pay for this someday," Martin replied as he boarded his bike and sped away.

"Jimmy," called Mother from the front door. "What happened? Is everything all right?"

"Things are just fine," Jimmy said proudly.

CHAPTER 8

TROUBLE BREWING

Chapter 8 – "Trouble Brewing"

"Honey, I really don't think Jimmy and I should go camping this year." Father impatiently told Mother.

"But dear, it's such an important time for you and your son," she said. "Jimmy has been looking forward to it all year."

"Now, let's be realistic. Ever since Lucky came to our home, Jimmy hasn't spent five minutes thinking about this trip. Matter of fact, I bet he's forgotten all about it."

"Now, come on. Do you really think that Jimmy would forget something as important to him as this? Besides, he'd only be away from Lucky for two days."

"That boy wouldn't leave that dumb bird for a minute."

"Honey!"

"Plus, even if we did go, all we'd ever talk about is Lucky, Lucky, Lucky."

"Dear, you sound like you're angry at Lucky."

"Angry? What do you mean?"

The doorbell interrupted their discussion. Father opened the door to the cool, summer night breeze.

In front of him stood a man in a blue uniform. It was a policeman.

"Can I help you?" Father asked cautiously.

"I'm Sergeant Hughes, Barstone County Police," the man said. "I'm here regarding your falcon..."

"You mean our hawk."

"Yes, your, ah, hawk. It seems that your hawk has viciously attacked and clawed a young man in this neighborhood."

Father's eyes grew concerned as Mother approached behind him.

"Are you talking about Martin Winslow?" Mother inquired.

"A Mr. and Mrs. Winslow reported that your hawk attacked their son two days ago in front of your house."

"That's not true," Mother said.

Sergeant Hughes continued. "In front of your house at approximately 2:00 pm. The hawk scratched the boy on the forearm and the back. The parents are understandably quite angry over the matter and are ready to press charges."

"Press charges!" Father exclaimed.

"Sergeant, this is a mistake." Mother said.

"I think there must be a perfectly good explanation," Father added.

"Well," Sergeant Hughes said, "there is sufficient evidence – with the wounds and all – and having a hawk in this neighborhood isn't the smartest pet to have, with all these children around."

"I'm sure we can explain everything," Father said.

"Well, explaining isn't going to do you any good here. You'll need to tell it to the judge. That is, unless..."

"Unless, what?" Mother asked.

"Well, the Winslow's are more concerned that this type of thing doesn't happen again. They're willing to drop charges if you both will –"

Jimmy appeared at the top of the stairs. "Who's at the door?"

"Just a minute, honey," Mother said. "We'll be done in a moment." She then turned to Sergeant Hughes and said softly, "If we'll what?"

"If you get rid of the hawk."

"No!" demanded Mother. "We can't."

"Honey," Father said. "We have a serious problem."

"Not as serious a problem as we'll have if Jimmy loses Lucky."

"Well, we need to --"

"Mom," Jimmy yelled. "I'm ready for bed now. Who's at the door?"

"Say your bedtime prayers, honey, and we'll be right there."

"Sir, ma'am," Sergeant Hughes said. "This is a serious matter. I suggest you accept the Winslow's offer and return the bird immediately. I don't think the judge will be very supportive of your case."

"Thank you, sir," Father replied. "We'll contact you shortly."

"But dear," Mother said through clenched teeth.

"We'll take care of the matter." Father assured Sergeant Hughes.

They exchanged goodbyes with the policeman and then closed the door. Mother was very upset.

"We cannot let Lucky go. Jimmy would be devastated."

"It's better than being in jail!" Father said. "Besides, it's time that Jimmy realizes that Lucky can't be his only friend in life."

"Before Lucky, Jimmy didn't have a friend. Now, you just go ahead and take him away."

"Listen. I've had enough! I'm going upstairs right now. Lucky has got to go!"

"Honey, I can't believe --"

"I've made up my mind. This is our only choice. I'll take care of it myself."

Mother stood amazed at Father's angry tone. She looked at him in complete shock as he stormed up the stairway to Jimmy's room. It was as if he really didn't like Lucky at all!

Father reached the top of the staircase to Jimmy's door and grabbed the knob. As soon as his hand touched the polished brass, a sudden chill hit him. He suddenly realized the difficulty of what he was about to do. He became strangely timid – even frightened – at the task at hand. He carefully, quietly, turned the doorknob.

Father peered inside Jimmy's room. As Mother requested, Jimmy was praying. Lucky, of course, was at his side, perched on the bed. Father could almost bet that Lucky's head was cuddled close to his left wing, as if he were praying too.

Father listened quietly.

"God, it's hard for me to not walk. It's not very much fun when all the kids are running around and playing, and I can't play with them. I know how poor Lucky must feel. So, God, I only ask you one thing, please make Lucky's wing better. Please make it so he can fly and be like the other hawks."

Father took a deep breath and entered the room. He had to face this task with courage. Jimmy's eyes opened as he turned to Father.

"Dad. Who was at the door?"

* * *

Mother waited at the base of the stairway. A few moments had passed, Father slowly walked down the steps. His downcast eyes would not dare connect with those of his wife.

"Well? What did you tell our son?" Mother asked.

Father looked up to Mother. His eyes told the whole story. He again took a deep breath and replied, "I told him we're going camping on Friday."

CHAPTER 9

STORM ADVISORY

Chapter 9 – "Storm Advisory"

Jimmy was finally finished packing. In just a few moments, he and his dad would be on their way to Devil's Mountain. Jimmy was excited to spend time away with his dad, but this time he was sorry to leave Lucky, even if it was for just two days.

"Don't worry, Lucky," Jimmy assured him. "I'll be back real soon. But I wish you could come with us. But Dad says no. Anyhow, Mom will take good care of you. I bet she'll even feed you the mice."

"Jimmy," called Mother. "Are you ready?"

* * *

Father positioned the tent into the back of the van. He glanced to the north to see once more the top of Devil's Mountain. He wondered again to himself, as he often did, whether this trip was safe for his son. They had gone there for three straight years, and there was never a problem. But still, it was not named Devil's Mountain for nothing.

Mother carried Jimmy down the short flight of stairs and all the way to the car.

"Mom, I can get there myself," Jimmy reasoned.

Mother kissed Jimmy on the cheek. "Oh, let your mother hold you a little longer before you're gone for the weekend."

"Are we all set?" Father inquired.

"You bet!" Jimmy replied.

"Now," Father said to Mother, "are you sure that you can settle this issue with Martin's parents?"

"Mrs. Winslow and I have known each other for ten years. Sure, we don't always see eye to eye, but –"

"Well, if there are any problems, call me on the cell phone and I'll come right down."

"You just concentrate on having fun with Jimmy. Now, let's see. You have the tent, the propane stove, clothes..."

"All right, we've already done this," Father said. "And we know that everything's here."

"And Jimmy's crutches?" Mother asked.

Father looked into the van's trunk. With a subtle face of embarrassment, he jogged into the house to retrieve the crutches.

"Now, you be good for your father," Mother said to Jimmy.

"I will," Jimmy said. "And will you take care of Lucky?"

"He's in good hands, kid. That is, as long as he doesn't mind strips of raw meat. No mice."

Jimmy smiled. Father returned to the car with the crutches, checked for the last time to ensure everything was packed, and kissed his wife.

"We're off," Father said triumphantly.

"Like a herd of turtles," Mother replied. "So long."

"Bye," Jimmy said. "Bye Lucky!"

A short squawk was heard from the upstairs window.

* * *

While thinking about what to do on her weekend alone with Lucky, Mother went back up to Jimmy's room to cover Lucky's cage. As she stood with the blanket in her hand, Mother peered out the window towards Devil's Mountain. She, too, felt a little nervous about that place, but they had never had any trouble before. She then glanced toward the east and noticed a small, dark cloud approaching. She checked in Jimmy's closet and let out a sigh.

"They forgot their umbrellas again."

* * *

The ride to Devil's Mountain was not long. But then again, no ride for a seven-year-old on vacation seems short.

"How much longer?" Jimmy asked.

"Son," Father replied. "we've only been driving for twenty minutes."

"Dad," Jimmy said excitedly, "look at that cloud!"

"Looks like rain."

"I'm sure glad we brought our umbrellas."

Father stared straight ahead. He did not say a word.

* * *

The last couple of miles up Devil's Mountain were the worst. Jimmy had to look straight ahead not to get car sick. Thinking about Lucky helped get his mind off the windy road.

Finally, the two arrived at their favorite spot. Father particularly liked this spot, hardly a soul ever visited this camp site and Father had never been fond of crowds. Jimmy peered out the passenger window to behold the beauty of this place. There were tall trees waving their limbs, flowered fields dancing up the sides of the peaks, and a stream running in the distance.

While Father busily pitched the six-man tent on a nearby flat, Jimmy positioned himself atop a small rock admiring the nature around him. Nothing could beat the fresh mountain air, accented with pine, or the bugs that scurried all around them. Jimmy thought of how much fun Lucky would have hunting them.

"Here it is," Father said triumphantly as the tent was completed. "Now time to go gather sticks for the fire."

"I'll go!" Jimmy replied excitedly.

Father thought for a moment. Last year, Jimmy volunteered to gather sticks, but had to return after a short while because he was tired. Father mulled it over quickly in his mind.

"Now, Jimmy. Are you sure you don't want me to come with you?"

"I'll be okay Dad. Please, let me go?"

Father nodded hesitantly. Jimmy went off beyond the nearby trees. The rain clouds they had seen earlier were quickly approaching overhead. Father called out to Jimmy, "Come back before it starts to rain."

"I will," Jimmy said, his voice muffled by the trees.

Jimmy had developed a pretty keen sense of direction. But to be careful, he intentionally pressed down hard on his crutches to leave a slight trail of dots that he could follow back to the campsite. Every couple of yards, Jimmy would find a stick, stop, place it under his right arm, press a dot into the dirt and move along. It began to get colder as the dark clouds moved overhead, and the tall trees didn't allow much light to come through. It was a little eerie for a young boy, but dad was only a short walk away. Besides, Jimmy wanted to be sure that, this time, he returned with plenty of sticks all by himself.

* * *

Father returned to the van to retrieve the propane stove. Reaching far into the car's trunk, he noticed the cell phone on the dashboard.

"Bet I forgot to turn it off," he told himself. He opened the driver's side door, reached for the phone, and turned it off.

Father turned the radio dial to the local news. The dark clouds had entirely engulfed the sky, and he wondered if he should go find his son.

"Again, the top story for this hour," the voice on the radio said, "A weather advisory has been issued for all of Barstone County and its surrounding areas. The season's first thunderstorm is expected to arrive within the hour."

I'll give him five more minutes, Father thought.

* * *

Jimmy was growing weary of all the difficult walking. He reminded himself to be persistent, since he only needed a few more sticks. Just then, his left crutch dug into a shallow hole which made him stagger ever so slightly. Jimmy quickly responded, he lunged into his other crutch to prevent himself from falling, dropping all the sticks to the ground. Jimmy regained his balance, slowly repositioned himself, and patiently picked the sticks back up.

A thunder peal screamed across the darkening sky. *I'd better get back*, Jimmy thought.

A cold, wet feeling ran across Jimmy's nose. The first raindrop had arrived. Jimmy was almost done gathering sticks, but he figured that enough was enough. He did not want to get caught in a rainstorm.

The thunder proclaimed that he was too late.

The driving rain began to drench the wooded area. Jimmy held tight to the sticks as he made his way back to the campsite. The darkness was now becoming less eerie and more frightening. "Just follow the dots," Jimmy kept reminding himself.

* * *

Back at home, Mother relaxed on the sofa and turned on the television with the remote control. The weatherman was giving his forecast.

"This large front is bringing on the summer's first storm. A weather advisory has been issued throughout all of Barstone County and its surrounding areas. Expect lightning and rain to hit no later than seven tonight."

Lightning and rain? Mother had to remind herself that everything would be okay. Still, she thought she'd better call her husband to let them know. She dialed her husband's cell phone to alert her family to stay near the campsite. Unfortunately, the phone rang again and again.

Oh well, Mother thought to herself. *They'll know about the storm in a couple of hours.*

Some time passed, and Mother tried to call Father again. This time, she got a familiar voice.

"Your call cannot be completed," said the recording.

Mother hung up the phone and wondered if she should make her way up to the mountain. She thought for a moment, then smiled, "Mothers do worry too much," she said to herself.

↓

CHAPTER 10

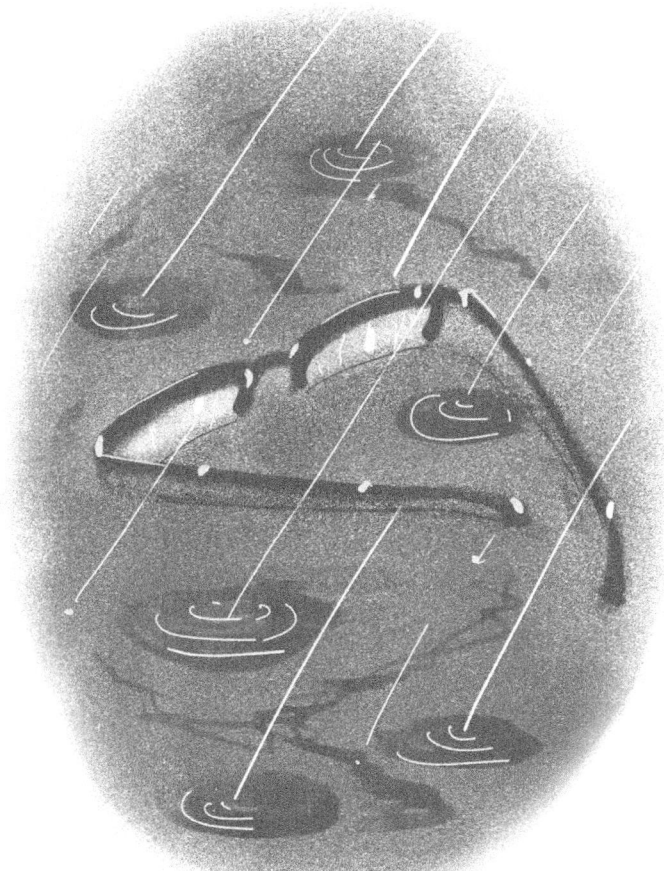

A NIGHTMARE
PART ONE

Chapter 10 – "A Nightmare" Part One

Mother gazed out the window of Jimmy's bedroom. The raindrops blurred her vision of Devil's Mountain as they trickled down the glass. Mother slowly backed away, only to bump into Lucky's covered cage. Lucky let out a startled cry.

"Oh!" Mother said, jumping back. She took the blanket off of Lucky's cage and commanded, "Don't ever frighten me like that again."

Lucky eyed back as if to say, "And don't ever frighten me like that again."

* * *

Jimmy kept following the dots back to the campsite. But, as the rain continued to beat upon the parched ground, the dots began to fade. Still, he followed them the best that he could. The sun had now descended below the trees and was fading behind the mountainside. Jimmy's heart began to beat violently as the darkness grew. The dots he had so carefully etched into the ground had totally vanished, he figured he could trust his own intuition, and decided to continue on.

Just then, something grabbed him from behind.

Jimmy screamed, lost his balance, and fell into the mud, the twigs scattering all about. Jimmy's glasses flung from his face and landed somewhere in the rain-soaked ground. Jimmy turned his head to see a low branch bouncing up and down, swaying in the wind. He peered forward into the now blackened woods. Jimmy could somewhat see without his glasses, though the blurred shapes would most definitely deceive him. The rocks to the side seemed to move along like creatures from a horrible nightmare. The trees glared back at him with evil eyes, as if to be waiting to fall upon him. Jimmy felt a tingling sensation up his back as figures in the dark fled past him.

"Dad! Help! I need you!" Jimmy called.

Jimmy found his way back to his feet and moved on ahead, not wasting time to search for his glasses, let alone the scattered twigs. The mud below made it difficult to walk with crutches, but fear moved Jimmy faster than ever before.

Jimmy continued feverishly though the dark forest, seeing shadowed creatures that frightened him at every turn. The sounds of owls and other animals kept Jimmy on constant guard. He no longer paid attention to where he was going. He only knew he wanted to get out.

The thunder and lightning continued to drown out Jimmy's cries for help. As the rain beat heavily upon his head, Jimmy realized now that he was lost. Finally, Jimmy grabbed hold of his whistle and blew.

But the storm silenced him.

Father tightened the hood of his coat and made his way toward the wooded area. He knew Jimmy couldn't be too far. Thinking he'd be gone for just a few minutes; he didn't even bother to carry the flashlight.

Several minutes passed, and Father grew scared. He knew he should have found Jimmy by now.

"Jimmy!" cried Father. "Jimmy! Do you hear me?"

He decided to hurry back to the camp site to retrieve the flashlight.

Father trudged through the thickening mud, waving the flashlight back and forth. He called Jimmy's name again and again, to no reply. He wondered if he should call for help. He decided that would take too long. So, he kept on, searching, praying, and calling out Jimmy's name.

* * *

Jimmy blew the whistle again and again. Each time, the wind, rain, and thunder seemed to triumph over him. Jimmy now had no idea where he was. He only knew that he needed to get out of the woods, and quick.

Suddenly, he saw light.

The sun was barely visible over the top of the faraway hillside. Still, Jimmy could see that the perimeter of the woods was in sight. He moved as fast as his crutches would allow toward the destination. He knew that if he got out of the woods, he could find his way back to the campsite. Jimmy's trembling hands held fast to his crutches, pushing himself along while his feet barely touched the ground. At last, he made it to the edge.

Jimmy looked around in the fading sunlight. He then noticed a faint light shining about a hundred yards away.

"Dad!" Jimmy yelled as he moved toward the light.

As Jimmy moved closer, the light continued away.

"Dad! This way!" Jimmy screamed, trying to yell over the pounding rain.

Jimmy went faster and faster, yelling to his father. Now in great fear, tears began to roll down Jimmy's face as the light continued to move away.

Finally, Jimmy grabbed for his whistle. He put the whistle to his lips and just as he prepared to blow, the crutches underneath him gave way. Jimmy's legs slid down and he fell upon his stomach. Only, now, he kept falling.

Jimmy screamed as he slid down the embankment of an unseen ledge. His fingers dug into the slimy mud to no avail as he continued down to the black beneath. Jimmy screamed louder and louder, sliding deeper and deeper. Suddenly, a large bush beneath the ledge braced his fall. Jimmy instinctively grabbed the thin branches with both hands and held on for dear life. The faint sunlight revealed his crutches falling down the deep gorge, at least one hundred feet below.

The light that pointed to Father could no longer be seen. The lightning raced, and the thunder cracked across the black sky. Jimmy cried and screamed in fear. Then, holding on as best as he could, Jimmy let go with one arm for the briefest moment and repositioned his whistle into his mouth. His arm began to slip down the soaked branches. Jimmy grabbed hold again with the other arm and braced himself against the side of the gorge. Jimmy knew he only had one chance, as best as his trembling lips would allow, Jimmy blew into the whistle, over and over again.

* * *

Suddenly, back at home, Lucky's eyes popped open. Something was wrong. He could hear it. Jimmy was in trouble!

CHAPTER 11

A NIGHTMARE
PART TWO

Chapter 11 – "A Nightmare" Part Two

In his cage upstairs, Lucky was squawking madly.

"Lucky, quiet!" Mother yelled from downstairs. But Lucky only screamed louder and louder.

Mother made her way up to the bedroom. She opened the door and stood silent. Lucky was screaming with all his might, and frantically moving back and forth in his cage.

"Jimmy will be back soon enough, you cry baby." Mother placed the blanket over the cage. As she walked toward the door, she heard a rattling sound.

Turning around, Mother saw the cage rocking back and forth. The blanket fell to the rug below. Her eyes widened as she watched Lucky jumping from one side of the cage to the other, frantically screaming.

"Lucky, what in the world?" Mother reached for the blanket and began to place it over the cage, when suddenly Lucky thrust his beak at her. Mother dropped the blanket and jumped back.

Lucky stopped his tirade, then gazed his piercing eyes into Mother's. Then, Lucky turned to face the window.

"Listen here, mister. You're not coming out of that cage."

Again, Lucky violently bounced the cage back and forth, screaming louder than ever. Mother edged back in fright when suddenly, the cage plummeted to the floor and its door swung open.

Mother jumped back to the opening of the door and watched as Lucky made his way out of the cage.

"What's wrong with you, Lucky?" yelled Mother.

Lucky positioned himself on the top of the cage and stared at Mother. His eyes were requesting her complete attention. Then, slowly, majestically, Lucky began to open his wings.

Both wings.

Mother looked at Lucky in utter shock as the hawk displayed himself in full glory. She did not know what to think except that, for some reason, Lucky could move his wing. His giant wingspan revealed itself for the first time, stretching over five feet! The diamond shape on his chest widened, stretched by the tight muscles of the once crippled hawk. Then, Lucky's eyes moved slowly to the window.

"No...no...oh no," Mother uttered, trembling. "There's no way I'm going to let you out."

Lucky's crowned head darted directly back at Mother. This time, his eyes demanded attention.

Mother felt the rush of fear overcome her. She tried to catch her breath as she quickly closed the door behind her and made her way down the stairs.

She didn't know what to do, but she had to do something. She would try to call Father again. She would call Mr. Siggy. She would –

A loud thump echoed from Jimmy's room.

Mother instantly ran back up the stairs, grabbed the doorknob, cracked open the door, and peered in. Lucky laid on the floor, dazed and staggered. A mark was left on the foggy window.

Mother looked on in silence and fear. Lucky made his way back to his feet, shook his head, and faced the window again. He then turned his head to the figure behind the door and let out that distinctive cry.

Mother's heart pounded louder than ever.

She remembered the sound of that cry.

"Dear God. It's Jimmy!"

Mother swung open the door and reached for the bedroom window. She flung open the window and turned to Lucky. She stared for an instant at the regal creature.

"I don't know what I'm doing, boy, but go get 'em!"

Lucky hopped to the window's ledge, revealed his full plumage, and escaped into the dark.

"What have I done?" she whispered.

Moments later, the phone started ringing, "Hello?" Mother franticly answered.

"Honey, it's Jimmy! He's lost in the woods. I've looked everywhere," Father's voice cracked with fear.

"Did you call 911?"

"The fire department is on their way. I can't believe I let this happen!"

"It's not your fault, Jimmy..." Mother paused, "That's why he was freaking out.... Honey, Lucky is on his way to help!"

"Oh, thank God. Lucky...Lucky?"

"I'll explain when I get there! I'm on my way!"

Mother jumped into her car and raced down the street. She sped downtown towards Highway 21 heading up to Devil's Mountain. The slick road was no match for a mother racing to rescue her son.

* * *

Father waited at the campsite, calling out Jimmy's name. He prayed that the fire department would arrive immediately.

* * *

Jimmy held tightly to the weakening branches, blowing the whistle over and over. He knew that as long as he could brace himself against the side of the gorge, he would be okay. But the rain was making it hard to hold on. He wondered if help would ever come.

* * *

Lucky fought against the violent wind and rain. He was not even adept at flying in calm weather, but sheer determination kept him sailing high above the valley floor. He moved closer towards the mountains, listening to the fearful sounds of the whistle. His muscles ached greatly, and his stamina was growing thin. But nothing was going to stop him.

CHAPTER 12

FOLLOW THAT HAWK

Chapter 12 – "Follow That Hawk!"

Lucky now soared high above Devil's Mountain. He continued forcefully toward the sound of the whistle. The keen eyes of the hawk could barely make out the shapes of trees, rocks, and a stream. Still, there was no sign of Jimmy.

Jimmy held tight to the branches. He could feel his grip loosening. He blew the whistle again. "God, help me," he prayed to himself. At that moment the whistle fell from his mouth.

Jimmy began to scream.

"Help! Help!" he cried again and again.

Jimmy called out with all his might, only to be silenced by the thunder above. The rain pressed hard against his frozen frame. He was losing hope.

A cracking sound drowned out the storm.

Jimmy screamed as he felt the bush starting to give way. He pressed hard against the cliff's side. The time was running short. He had to grab the whistle again.

Jimmy knew that one false move could mean death. He tried to let go with one hand, but fear constrained him. The branches began to sag further.

As instinct took over, Jimmy quickly reached for another branch. This time, the branch would hold.

A rush of relief raced through his body. He felt secure - for the moment. Now, he must get his whistle.

Jimmy slowly removed his right hand. He was holding steady. He quickly put the whistle back into his mouth and reached back toward the branches. Jimmy whistled as loud as he could.

Suddenly, a frightening figure appeared from above.

"Go away!" Jimmy screamed as the whistle settled back down to his chest.

Jimmy screamed in fright as the figure flew towards him, then he stopped gazed in amazement.

"Lucky, it's you! I knew you could fly! I knew you could!"

Lucky landed next to Jimmy and moved close to him, digging his talons deep in the mud.

"Lucky," Jimmy said. "Go get dad! I need help! Go find dad!"

Lucky spread his fearsome wings and darted off into the night.

Jimmy held on fast to the branches, a ray of hope keeping his grip firm. Jimmy was aching all over. He could feel his wet hands begin to burn. He wondered if the warm trickle down his arm was rain or blood.

* * *

The lights of the fire truck could be seen in the distance. Father waved the flashlight to and fro to signal them. The truck made its way up the road and stopped at the camp site. Father ran to the driver.

"My son, he's lost in the woods. He's on crutches..."

"We'll have our men search the entire area, sir," the driver replied, turning to his companions. "Make sure to grab plenty of rope."

"Rope?" Father asked.

"Sir, there are cliffs and gorges all about the perimeter of these woods. The first thing we need to do is make sure that your son hasn't fallen off the side."

Father stood motionless, frightened. Suddenly, he heard a familiar sound.

"Lucky?" Father whispered to himself.

Lucky flung down and landed at the feet of Father. A fireman nearby jumped back startled in fear.

"Lucky! Do you know where he is? Where's Jimmy?"

Lucky extended his wings and took off toward the woods.

"Follow him," Father pointed. "That hawk!"

"What in the world?" the fire captain asked.

"Please. Don't ask questions. Just follow that hawk."

Two firemen with ropes scurried through the mud as Father followed. Lucky blazed over the trees, staying within sight and earshot of the men below.

"He's headed toward Devil's Gorge," said one of the firemen.

Lucky continued on, screaming away.

* * *

The car slid to a stop, almost taking out a fireman and nearly slamming into the firetruck. Mother opened the door.

"What's the matter with you, lady?" yelled a fireman.

"I'm the boy's mother. Have you found him?"

"Your husband told our guys to follow him. He was chasing after some bird."

"Which way did they go?"

The fireman pointed into the woods. Mother hurried off into the dark.

* * *

The firemen continued racing toward Lucky. They then burst through the perimeter of the trees and watched as the hawk descended into Devil's Gorge.

"Tie down your rope!" yelled one of the men.

Lucky landed beside Jimmy. Jimmy was relieved to see him again.

"Lucky, where's Dad?" Jimmy moaned.

Just then, a rope flung past Jimmy's face.

"Son! Grab the rope," a man said from above.

Jimmy's weariness turned to strength as he reached his left arm toward the rope. Suddenly, he heard a cracking sound. The branch broke.

Jimmy screamed.

Jimmy grabbed the rope with his left hand but continued to slide down. Then, suddenly he stopped. He felt something tugging at his sleeve. Lucky was holding Jimmy's arm by his beak, barely grasping the bush with his talons.

"Hold on Jimmy!" Father screamed in terror.

"I can't! I'm gonna fall!"

"Grab the rope with both hands!" shouted the fireman.

As if he understood every word, Lucky spread his wings. He took to the air and flung Jimmy's right arm toward the rope. Jimmy now held the rope with both hands.

"Hold on kid. We're going to bring you up."

Just then Mother arrived. She raced over to Father and peered down the ledge.

"Jimmy!" she screamed.

"We've got him, ma'am," one of the men replied. "We'll get him up."

Lucky hovered over Jimmy as the firemen began to pull him to the ledge. He was about thirty feet away from the top. Suddenly, he felt his hands slipping.

"Brace yourself!" a fireman yelled.

The firemen knew they had little time left. They threw down a second rope, and one of the men began to climb toward Jimmy.

"I'm falling!" Jimmy yelled.

"Don't worry, Jimmy. I'll be right there. You just hold on," the descending fireman yelled.

Lucky saw the man climbing down, settling next to Jimmy, Lucky looked Jimmy in the eyes.

"Lucky, I can't make it," Jimmy said, sobbing, his body drenched by the freezing rain. Lucky glared deeper into Jimmy's eyes.

"I'm coming kid. Hold on!" hollered the fireman.

Jimmy looked at Lucky as his hands slid ever so slightly. Then, he realized what he was saying.

"Lucky, you didn't give up. You learned to fly. I can do it too."

Jimmy grabbed onto the rope so tightly that he was sure that the twine was cutting through his skin.

The fireman was only about ten feet above him. He was going to make it.

Then, a crumbling sound. The fireman yelled, "Whoa!" as he slipped to the side. A large boulder beneath him came loose from the muddy wall. It was tumbling down towards Jimmy.

The sound of the crashing boulder echoed throughout the rain-soaked pit. No other sound was heard from below.

"Lucky!" screamed Jimmy.

Jimmy began sobbing uncontrollably.

Just then, the fireman reached over and grabbed him.

"I'm here now, son. Everything's okay. You're fortunate that the bird saved you from the rock."

"But where's Lucky?" Jimmy's voice was broken by shock and tears.

"You mean the bird? I'm sorry, son, but he's gone."

Jimmy was hoisted above the ledge and into the arms of his parents. Tears of joy from Mother and Father could not override the tears of pain from Jimmy.

"Jimmy. Thank God you're okay," Mother sobbed.

Jimmy buried his head into Mother's bosom.

"Mommy," Jimmy said between sobs, "the man said... I was fortunate. I thought fortunate meant... lucky."

CHAPTER 13

SHATTERED DREAMS

Chapter 13 – "Shattered Dreams"

Father carried Jimmy up the stairs to his bedroom. When they entered through the door, Lucky's large, empty cage stared back at them.

Father laid the cold and crying boy into his bed.

"We'll see Dr. Ambers tomorrow to make sure you're okay. Is that a deal?" Father said kindly. Jimmy lay quietly, the only sounds being his occasional sobs as he stared at the cage. Father glanced at the perch where Lucky would stand. He turned to Jimmy.

"Do you want me to take this away?"

"No," Jimmy said urgently. "Lucky's gonna come back. And I want to be sure that he has a place to stay when he does."

Just then, Mother entered. "Honey," she said, "why don't you just get some rest. We'll talk more in the morning."

"But Lucky is coming back, right, Mom?"

"Son," Father said, "Lucky fell a long way. And..."

"And we'll talk about it later," Mother interrupted. "Now you just get to sleep."

Mother and Father each kissed Jimmy and left the room.

"I don't know what to say," Father said to her. "Lucky meant so much to him."

"What is there to say?" Mother replied. "Sure, it's going to hurt. But Jimmy's endured enough tonight..." Mother began to weep.

Father put his arms around his wife and led her downstairs.

Jimmy laid silent in bed, listening to the rain beat against the window blackened by the night. The image of a boulder crushing his best friend was constantly replaying in his head. Sleep was the farthest thing from his mind.

Then, something broke the silence.

Scratch. Scratch. Scratch.

Jimmy's heart raced. His moist eyes lit up. He knew that sound. It was the sound of talons scratching against the window sill.

"Mom! Dad! Hurry!" Jimmy shouted.

Father and Mother burst through the door.

"What's wrong!" Father cried.

"It's Lucky!" Jimmy yelled.

Father looked at Mother. They both turned toward the window when they heard the scratching noise.

"Quick! Open the window! The window!" Jimmy screamed.

Father quickly dashed toward the rain pounded window. Mother waited in anxious anticipation. Her hands covering her mouth. Jimmy lifted his torso to a seated position, ready to receive his friend. Father opened the window.

A sudden scurry broke the silence. A tired, wet pigeon, seeking shelter from the rain, flew off in fright. Without saying a word, Father shut the window.

Jimmy's heart sank.

Mother, fighting back her tears, gently tucked Jimmy back into bed. The room darkened once again. Jimmy whispered to himself "Looks like I really am a pigeon boy."

CHAPTER 14

A CONFESSION

Chapter 14 – "A Confession"

"Yes, Mrs. Winslow. With what happened last night, I can assure you that no other child will be attacked by our hawk again. Yes, and thank you. Goodbye." Mother hung up the phone and glanced at the sunlight peering through the kitchen window. It wasn't how she planned it, but at least the Winslow's would no longer press charges against their family. Father came down the stairs.

"How is he?" Mother asked.

"He must've been up real late, because he's still sound asleep," Father replied. "He's always up by this time in the morning."

"I talked to Mrs. Winslow. Everything is cleared up now."

"Everything? I think our problems have only begun. As soon as Jimmy realizes that Lucky isn't coming back, he'll be devastated."

"I called Dr. Ambers. He couldn't fit us in until tomorrow afternoon."

"That's probably for the better. The poor child doesn't need anything else to worry about."

Just then, the pesky little mouse darted across the kitchen floor and disappeared underneath the refrigerator. Mother didn't even flinch.

"I guess it's our job to catch that mouse," Mother replied.

* * *

Meanwhile, at the Winslow's. Mrs. Winslow called for Martin, "Son, we've got something to tell you."

Mr. and Mrs. Winslow pulled Martin away from the morning cartoons and sat him down on the family room couch.

Martin's mother spoke first. "We just talked to Jimmy's Mom. It seems that there was a terrible accident last night, and their bird died."

"He won't be bothering you any longer," Martin's Dad said. He then went to tell the story of what happened.

Martin sat in silence. His eyes began to well up with tears.

"Martin," said his mother, "what's the matter?"

Martin continued to sit still. After a few moments he spoke. "I lied. Lucky never attacked me. It was all made up. I was mad at Jimmy because all the kids liked him more than me. I'm sorry."

Martin's parents stared at him in disbelief.

"Get your jacket on," demanded his mother. "We're going to Jimmy's house."

* * *

The doorbell rang. Father peered through the peephole. He let out a deep sigh. It was the Winslow's.

Father slowly opened the door. "Mr. and Mrs. Winslow, Martin, what a surprise. Didn't my wife just talk to you?"

"Don't worry about a thing," Mr. Winslow said. "We brought Martin over to tell you something. Martin, say what you need to say."

Martin remained silent. Mother made her way to the door to see what was going on.

"Martin," Mrs. Winslow said sternly.

"I'm sorry," Martin said.

"Continue," Mr. Winslow said. Jimmy's parents remained still and quiet.

"I'm sorry I lied," Martin said.

"About what?" Father asked

"About Lucky. Lucky never did anything to me. I made it all up. I really feel bad about the whole thing. Can I talk to Jimmy?"

"Jimmy's been through a lot," said Mother. "I really don't want to disturb him now."

Father bent down to speak to Martin. "Martin, I'm glad you told us this. It took a lot of courage to say what you said."

"Oh, he knows what would happen if he didn't tell you," Mr. Winslow replied.

Father asked, "Martin, why did you do it?"

Martin looked down at the cement porch. He spoke softly. "I was jealous."

"I sort of know how you felt," Father said. "I was a little jealous of Lucky too. For a while, I kind of wished he wasn't here at all. Now that he's gone, I don't know what we're going to do."

Martin began to cry.

Father stood up and thanked the Winslow's. Mrs. Winslow offered her sympathy. As the Winslow's made their way back to the sidewalk, Martin turned around. He wasn't crying anymore. "Did Lucky really fly?" he asked.

Mother walked outside and put her hands upon his cheeks.

"Not only did Lucky fly," she said, "but he also saved Jimmy's life."

"Then why didn't he fly before?"

Mother thought for a moment. "I really don't know. Maybe he never had a reason."

CHAPTER 15

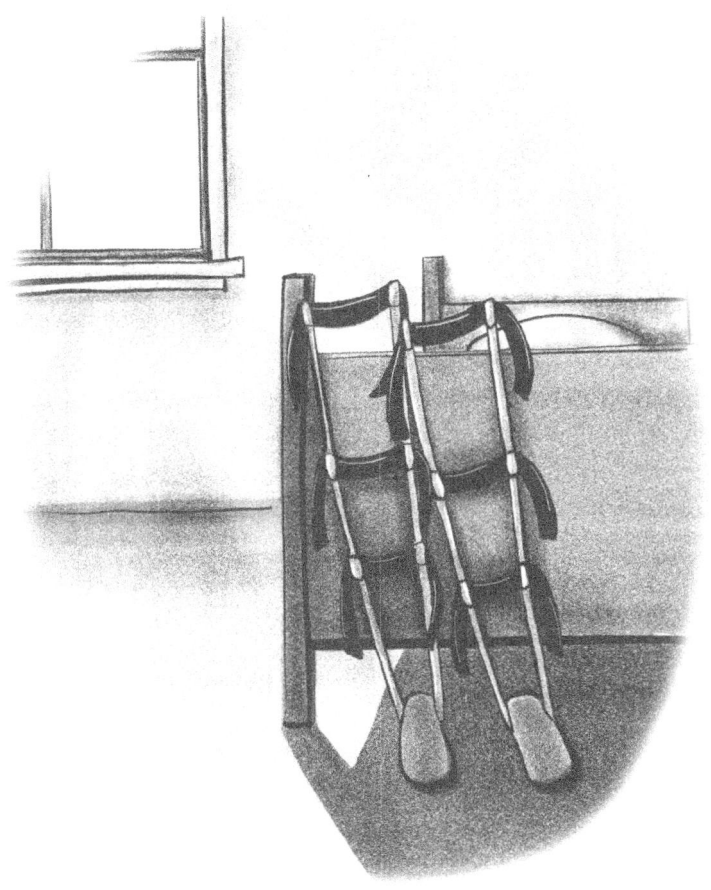

A DREAM COME TRUE

Chapter 15 – "A Dream Come True"

Jimmy was dreaming about Lucky. As always, he dreamed that Lucky was flying. The neighborhood kids would all run toward the majestic hawk as he soared as high as the clouds, disappearing into the afternoon sky, then sailing back down with blistering speed. Jimmy of course, would laugh and cheer. It was like all the dreams he had before. Only this time, one thing was different. One very important thing.

Startled, Jimmy's eyes popped open.

Half asleep, half awake, Jimmy thought he heard a sound.

Scratch. Scratch.

Jimmy blinked his eyes to clear the spider webs from his mind. Still, the sound continued.

Scratch. Scratch.

Jimmy had heard that sound before. Yet, only last night, his dreams were shattered. This time, though, another sound caught him by surprise.

"Squawk!"

Jimmy quickly found his way to the window, and with all his strength slid the glass pane open. He peered his head through and saw nothing.

Jimmy closed his eyes in despair. He placed his hands back onto the sliding glass window ready to shut his dreams forever.

"Squawk! Squawk!"

Out of the dark, a feathered shadow blazed through the open entrance into Jimmy's room. A majestic bird landed on top of the bed. Jimmy looked in shock. He held his composure for a moment to be sure he was awake. He blinked one last time. He was not dreaming.

Lucky was back!

Jimmy screamed, "Lucky! Lucky!... Mom! Dad! Hurry!"

Father flung the door open. Their eyes widened as they saw a soiled room, a filthy boy, and a blackened bird saturated in mud.

"Look, Mom! Look, Dad! It's Lucky!"

"I can't believe it!" Father yelled. "This is a miracle. It really is Lucky."

"He came back, Dad. I knew he'd come back." said Jimmy.

Father began to cry when he saw the joy in his son's eyes. He went to the window to give Jimmy a hug. Lucky paced back and forth upon the bed, as if he too wanted a hug. Mother stood motionless at the door while embracing her heart.

"Honey, are you okay?" Father asked.

"Don't worry about the mud, Mommy," Jimmy said. "Lucky and I will clean it up."

Obviously shaken, Mother muttered something under her breath.

"What's the matter?" Father asked again.

Mother stared at Jimmy and said, "Your braces. They're still by your bedside."

Jimmy, Father, and Lucky all peered down to the side of Jimmy's bed. His braces still stood tall and untouched from the night before.

Father let go of Jimmy. Confused and shaken from the sudden rush of the moment, he stepped back and stared at his son.

"Jimmy," he asked. "How did you get to the window?"

Jimmy shared the same look of confusion. He held tight to the window sill, then looked down to his knees. There were no shiny, steel braces hiding his bare legs. He held onto nothing but the window sill, a short walk from his bed. He turned to his Mother.

"I was dreaming that I could walk."

"Honey," Mother said slowly, dropping down to her knees. She held out her arms and opened her hands, "Come here."

Jimmy stood still. He looked around the room and saw the mud splattered upon the walls. He turned to his father. Jimmy had seen that look before, but always when something terrible had happened. He then turned to Lucky. The piercing eyes of Jimmy's best friend spoke louder than anyone in the room. His eyes shared something that only this special little seven-year-old boy with freckles and red hair could understand. These eyes blared a message that resounded inside Jimmy's head. They spoke only a single word: *Fly!*

Jimmy slowly lifted his left leg. He staggered ever so slightly. He held tight to the window sill as he gently positioned his right leg in front. There were feelings and sensations in his legs that he had never felt before. There was also a balance he never imagined except in his dreams.

Jimmy turned one last time to Lucky and looked at his mother.

Jimmy let go of the window sill.

His left leg inched forward. His right leg followed. Father stared in utter silence. Mother swallowed deep as joyful tears made their way down her cheeks. Jimmy lunged himself into Mother's arms.

"I walked, Mommy! I walked!" Jimmy sobbed as he flung his arms around her neck.

"Thank you. Thank you," Mother said looking up, her voice barely breaking the tears.

Father joined in for a group hug with tears streaming down his cheeks, saying over and over, "It's a miracle."

Lucky spread his wings and leaped from the bed to the top of his cage. He let out a triumphant cry that echoed out of the bedroom and resounded down the entire block. For him, knowing Jimmy could walk was greater than knowing he could fly. Of course, for Jimmy, seeing Lucky spread his wings was the greatest sight in the world. Together, they shared a dream come true.

"Lucky!" Jimmy proclaimed. "We can fly!"

* * *

That next school year, Jimmy became the talk of the entire playground. And every afternoon, as the children would return to their homes, each would take the route past the house of Jimmy, the red-haired boy who learned to walk, to behold the majestic site of the stoic hawk perched on the windowsill. Of course, Lucky was the talk of the neighborhood too, since there was not a mouse within miles of that home.

Except for one.

THE END

THANK YOU

Without you, our readers,
the dream of Lucky soaring would not have
been able to come true.

Please write us an online review and tell us
what you thought of Lucky.

Check us out on Facebook
Lucky- A Child's Dream Come True
Or online at
www.luckythehawk.com

ABOUT THE AUTHOR

Stephen would tell his daughter, Danielle, a new story almost every night that she stayed with him. Every story would start with a scary wind noise and end with a wonderful *happily ever after*. Even when his daughter would fall asleep half way though, he would have to finish his own story just to know what happened. After many years of telling these stories, Stephen finally decided to put one on paper. With the help with his siblings, Stephen turned his story about Lucky into a book. Over 20 years later, with the help of his Daughter and Son-in-Law, Stephen is finally getting his book out there to share his story about Lucky to the world.

Stephen currently lives in Brentwood, California with his daughter Danielle, her husband Clarence, and their two wild boys, Oliver and CJ. He loves watching movies, investigating toy car crashes, and still tells stories to his grandsons upon request.

Made in the USA
Las Vegas, NV
15 April 2022

47523697R00073